Animal Babies

Across
1. Baby chicken (5)
3. Baby pig (6)
5. Baby deer (4)
6. Baby bear (3)
8. Baby horse (4)

Down
2. Baby cat (6)
3. Baby dog (3)
4. Baby sheep (4)
6. Baby cow (4)
7. Baby kangaroo (4)

Time's Up!

puzzle 2

Across
3. This clock hand goes round the fastest (6)
4. 24 hours make one of these (3)
5. There are seven days in one of these (5)
6. This many minutes in an hour (5)
7. The small hand on a clock tells this (4)

Down
1. Typically about four weeks long (5)
2. Ten years (6)
5. Wrist, pocket or smart (5)

Stellar Solar System

puzzle 3

Across
2. The name of our galaxy (5,3)
4. This planet has lots of rings (6)
6. This planet rotates on its side (6)
7. The only planet to rotate clockwise (5)

Down
1. Also known as the Blue Planet (5)
2. The smallest planet in our solar system (7)
3. Known as the Red Planet (4)
4. Jupiter's storm is known as the Red what? (4)
5. Named after the Roman god of the sea (7)

Incredible Insects

puzzle 4

Across
1. Kept by an apiarist in a hive (4)
3. Fire, garden, carpenter and pharaoh are all types of this creature (3)
4. This insect chirps by rubbing its wings together (7)
6. These high jumpers make your dog scratch (4)
7. An expert flier that can't breath fire (9)

Down
1. Was once a caterpillar (9)
2. You might find this insect praying (6)
5. It has yellow and black stripes and can sting you (4)

Special Shapes

puzzle 5

Across
2. A 3D circle (6)
4. Can have a square or triangular base (7)
6. Ice cream goes with this shape (4)
7. Cereal box shaped (6)

Down
1. You might find this shape in a circus! (9)
3. A sort of tube (8)
5. Looks like a diamond (7)
7. Sugar can come in this shape (4)

Body

puzzle 6

Across
2. These carry blood back to your heart (5)
6. These might knock if you're afraid (5)
7. This pump has valves and chambers (5)
8. Bony protection for your brain (5)
9. Enables you to bend your arm (7)

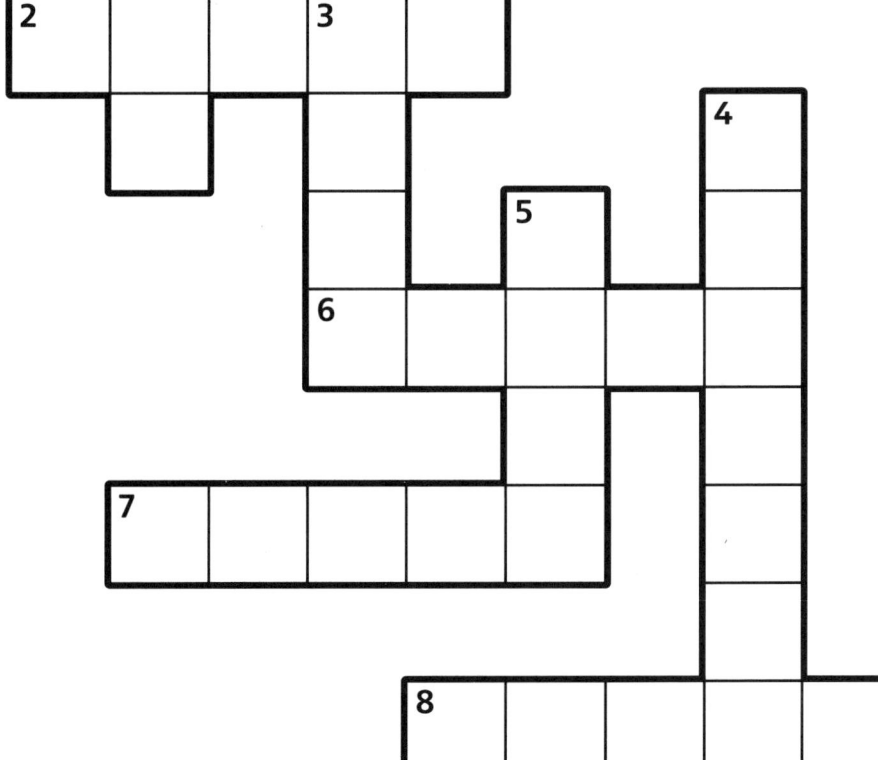

Down
1. Index, ring or little (7)
3. You can crane it, or put it on the line (4)
4. Air – and smells – go in here (7)
5. You walk and kick with these (4)
8. Organ that digests food (7)

Wild World

puzzle 7

Across
1. When Earth's plates move and shake (10)
3. Sometimes called a 'twister' (7)
4. A destructive tidal wave (7)
8. To leave a place of danger (8)

Down
2. A fearsome storm (9)
5. An explosive mountain (7)
6. A flash before thunder (9)
7. A very dry period (7)

Dinosaurs

puzzle 8

Across
3. Small carnivore that moved swiftly on two legs (12)
6. A plant eater with a long tail and neck (10)
7. The king of the dinosaurs (1,3)

Down
1. Has three horns, and a bony frill on its neck (11)
2. Feathered, flying dinosaur (13)
4. A fan of spines run down its back (11)
5. This herbivore has bony plates along its back and tail (11)

Vegetable Matters

puzzle 9

Across
1. Don't put this in a bouquet! (11)
3. Makes tasty pies and fun lanterns (7)
5. Bugs Bunny likes to eat these (7)
6. Looks like small, green trees (8)

Down
2. Has many layers (5)
3. Mash, bake, roast or fry this vegetable (6)
4. You'll find these in a pod (4)
6. Runner, green and broad are all types of ___ (5)

Continents

puzzle 10

Across
2. Cantonese, Malay and Thai are some of the languages spoken on this continent (4)
4. You'd find the Rocky Mountains here (5,7)
6. The largest island in the world, this country is also the name of a continent (9)

Down
1. Where would you find world's longest mountain range? (5,7)
2. The Sahara Desert is on this continent (6)
3. The most southerly continent (10)
5. Vatican City, the smallest country in the world, is found on this continent (6)

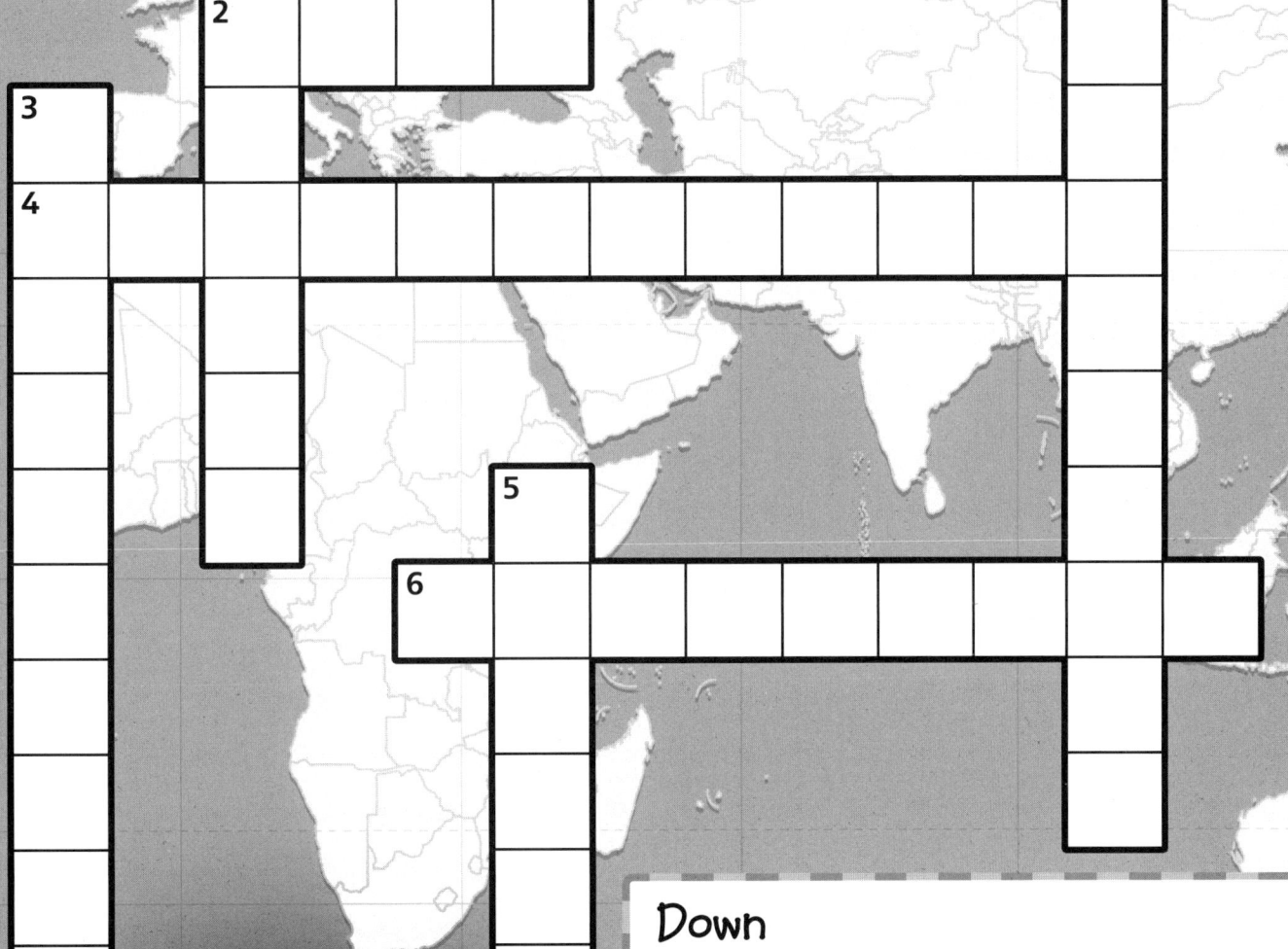

Months of the Year

Across
2. You might think this was the seventh month (9)
4. The last month with 30 days (8)
6. The eighth month of the year (6)
9. ___ O'Neil, friend of the Ninja Turtles (5)
10. Named after Julius Caesar, who was born in this month (4)

Down
1. The shortest month of the year (8)
3. This month is named after the Roman god of war, Mars (5)
5. Pumpkins and ghouls are associated with this month (7)
7. How many months there are in a year (6)
8. Auld Lang Syne is sung at the start of this month (7)

Number Hunt

puzzle 12

Across
3. Multiply the blind mice by Goldilocks's bears (4)
4. Letters in the alphabet (6-3)
5. *Around the World in __ Days* (6)
7. Henry VIII had this many wives (3)

Down
1. The first moon landing was in 19__ (5-4)
2. Snow White's dwarfs (5)
4. The Duke of York had 10 __ men (8)
6. __ green bottles (3)

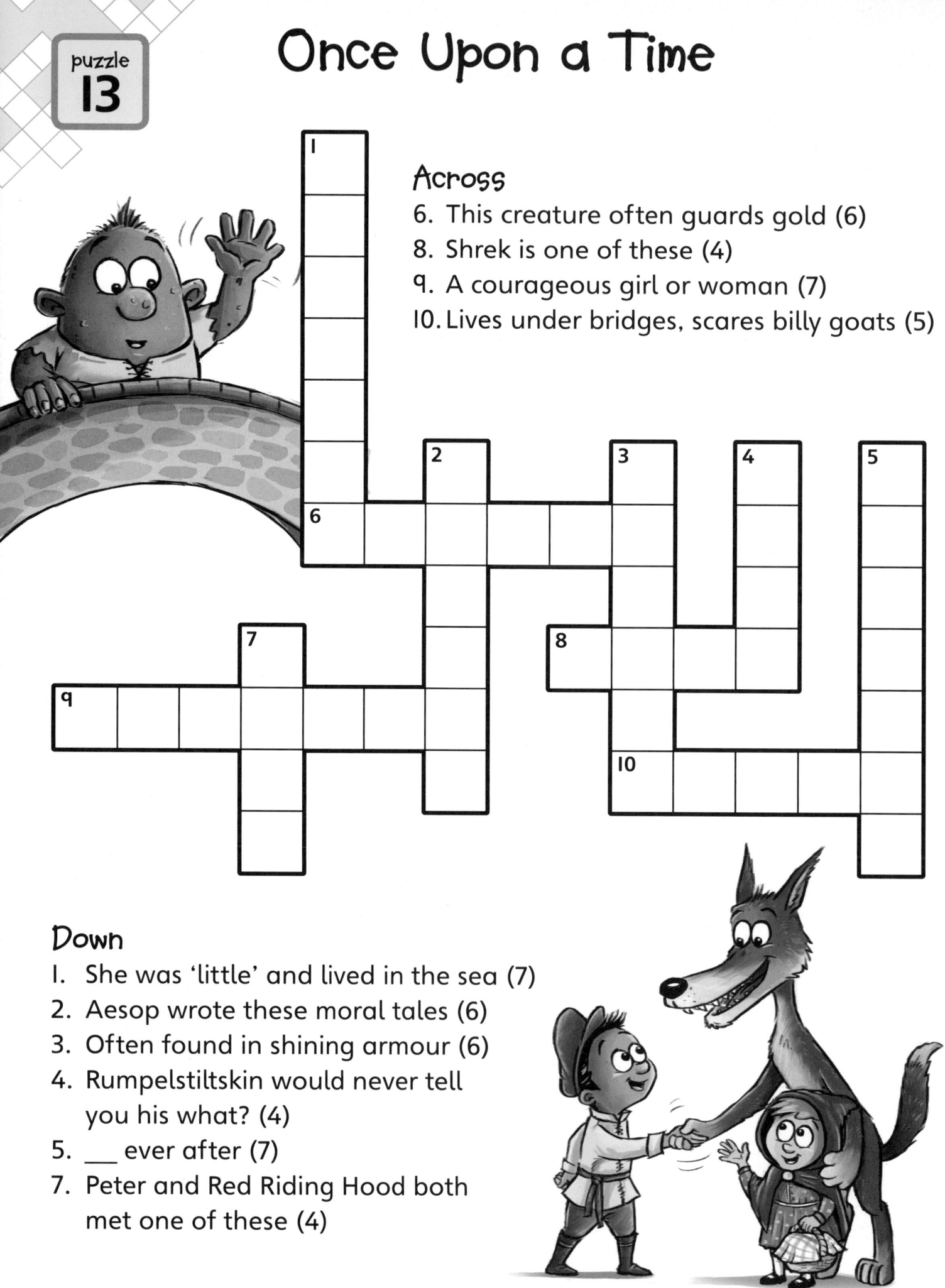

Once Upon a Time

puzzle 13

Across
6. This creature often guards gold (6)
8. Shrek is one of these (4)
9. A courageous girl or woman (7)
10. Lives under bridges, scares billy goats (5)

Down
1. She was 'little' and lived in the sea (7)
2. Aesop wrote these moral tales (6)
3. Often found in shining armour (6)
4. Rumpelstiltskin would never tell you his what? (4)
5. ___ ever after (7)
7. Peter and Red Riding Hood both met one of these (4)

Out of This World

puzzle 14

Across
3. Shooting stars (7)
7. Launches astronauts into space (6)
8. This Stephen studied black holes (6)

Down
1. A planet's path around the Sun (5)
2. What light years are a measurement of (8)
4. Which travels faster, light or sound? (5)
5. Sir Isaac Newton discovered this (7)
6. Of the Moon (5)
9. Ours is called the Milky Way (6)

Plant Parts

puzzle 15

Across
2. The uppermost part of a forest (6)
4. Trees often have lots of these (8)
7. A flower's 'trunk' (4)
8. Plants 'breathe' through these (6)

Down
1. A tree's protective skin (4)
3. Tiny grains collected by bees (6)
5. These grow into the ground (5)
6. Colourful part of a flower (5)

Quizzical Countries

puzzle 16

Across
1. Home to the Olympics, the Minotaur and the Parthenon (6)
3. Home of bagpipes, kilts and the Loch Ness monster (8)
4. The maple leaf is the national symbol here (6)
6. The home of the Vikings (6)
7. The land of the rising sun (5)

Down
1. A colourful country (9)
2. This country is shaped like a boot (5)
5. Land Down Under (9)

The Ends of the Earth

puzzle 17

Across
2. Polar bears live here (6)
4. The ends of the Earth (5)
6. The Earth ___ on its axis (7)

Down
1. Colourful light display in the sky (6)
3. Dangerous to ships in icy waters (7)
4. These Antarctic birds can't fly (7)
5. There's no land at this pole (5)

Around the World

puzzle 18

Across
2. Which is the saltiest sea? (4)
5. You'd find giant pandas here (5)
7. Mount ___ is the highest mountain in the world (7)
8. The Grand ___ is in North America (6)
9. The largest country in the world (6)

Down
1. In which city is the Eiffel Tower? (5)
3. Island with large stone heads (6)
4. Home of the Great Pyramid of Giza (5)
6. Victoria Falls is in this continent 6)
9. Uluru is also known as Ayers ___ (4)

The World's Oceans

puzzle 19

Across
1. The movement of water (7)
5. Also known as 'The Pond' (8)
6. High, low, rip, spring (4)
7. The Maldives and Sri Lanka are found in this ocean (6)

Down
1. A sailor might use this to navigate (7)
2. You'll find penguins in this ocean (8)
3. The largest ocean (7)
4. Very cold at the top of the world (6)

Awesome Adventures

puzzle 21

Across
2. A map and compass help you do this (8)
6. Roald ___, leader of first expedition to reach the South Pole (8)
7. Edmund ___, first to reach the summit of Everest (7)
8. The ___ brothers, inventors of the first aeroplane (6)

Down
1. Neil ___, first man on the Moon (9)
3. A journey made by explorers and adventurers (10)
4. Ferdinand ___, the first person to circumnavigate the globe (8)
5. Amelia ___, the first woman to fly solo across the Atlantic (7)

Landmarks

puzzle 22

Across
2. Could you eat your dinner at this mountain in South Africa? (5)
7. The Taj Mahal is in this country (5)
8. Prehistoric stone circle in England (10)

Down
1. The Leaning Tower of ___ (4)
3. The Golden Gate ___ is in San Fransisco (6)
4. A famous bell in London (3,3)
5. Where you'd find the Great Wall (5)
6. The Statue of ___ stands in New York Harbour (7)

Fragile World

puzzle 23

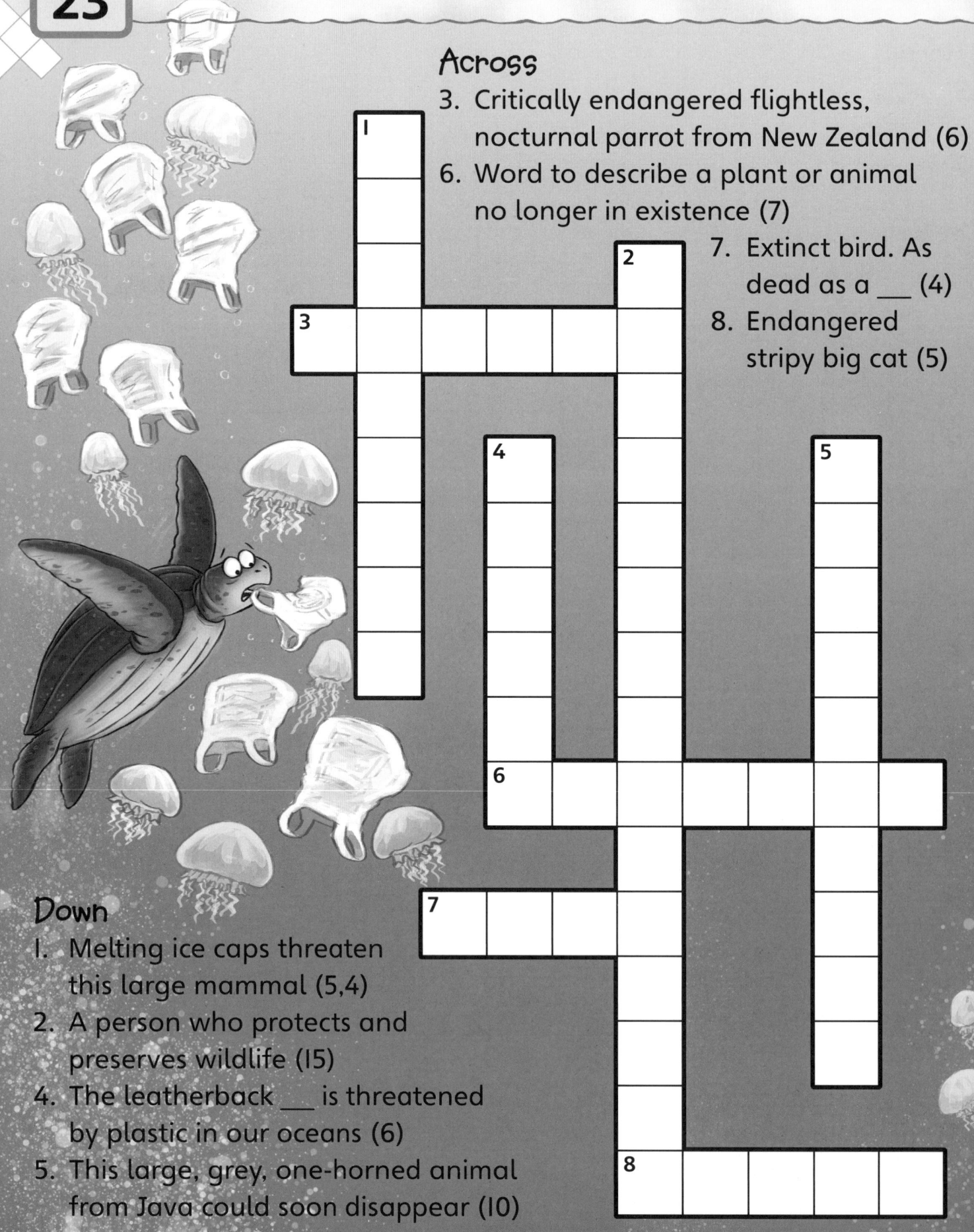

Across
3. Critically endangered flightless, nocturnal parrot from New Zealand (6)
6. Word to describe a plant or animal no longer in existence (7)
7. Extinct bird. As dead as a ___ (4)
8. Endangered stripy big cat (5)

Down
1. Melting ice caps threaten this large mammal (5,4)
2. A person who protects and preserves wildlife (15)
4. The leatherback ___ is threatened by plastic in our oceans (6)
5. This large, grey, one-horned animal from Java could soon disappear (10)

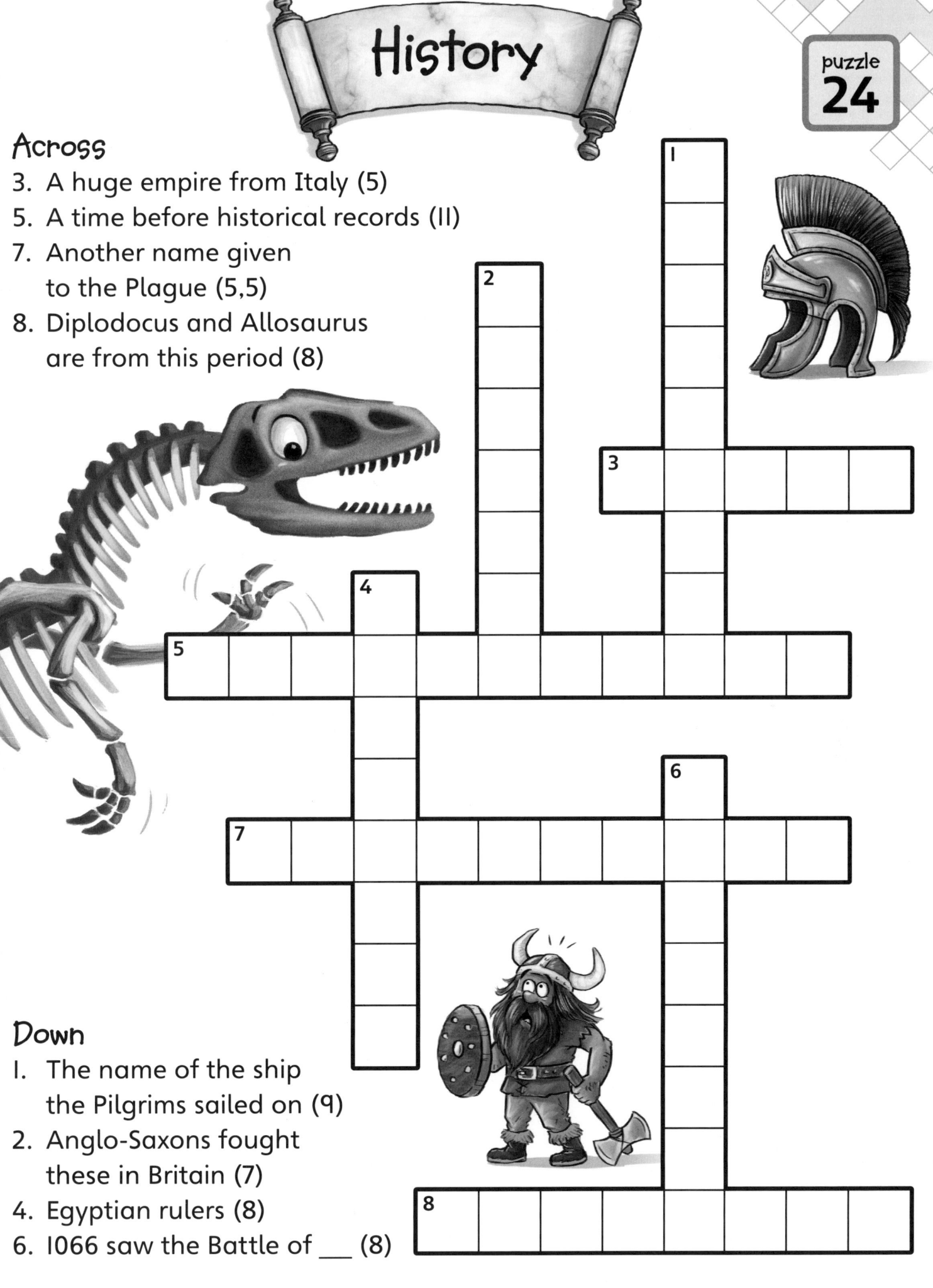

The Water Cycle

puzzle 26

Across
2. The layer of gases surrounding the Earth (10)
4. A pool of liquid on the ground or floor (6)
6. A common form of precipitation (4)
7. Transpiration is when a plant does this (8)
8. Fine water droplets in the air (4)

Down
1. Vapour becomes liquid when it ___ (5)
3. Turn liquid into vapour (9)
5. These carry water to the ocean (6)

Rulers of the World

puzzle 27

Across
2. A 'Great' king from ancient Greece (9)
6. George ___, the first president of the United States (10)
7. Last name of first black president of the USA (5)

Down
1. The last pharoah of Egypt (7)
3. Leader of the Hun army (6)
4. Surname of the first female British prime minister (8)
5. English king (VIII) with six wives (5)
6. Queen Elizabeth II is from the House of ___ (7)

Where Things Come From

puzzle 28

Across
1. Where does beef come from? (4)
2. What creature makes silk? (4)
3. What do chickens lay? (4)
5. Where does cotton come from? (6)
7. This is made from milk (6)

Down
1. What do we make from cocoa beans? (9)
4. The Olympic Games first began in this country (6)
6. Where does paper come from? (5)

Water in the Air

puzzle 29

Across
3. Hard, frozen water droplets (4)
6. Fog mixed with smoke and other pollutants (4)
8. Made when sunlight shines through water droplets (7)

Down
1. Vapour caused by heating liquid (5)
2. Cumulus, cirrus or stratus, for example (6)
4. Liquid that has evaporated (6)
5. Water droplets on the inside of windows (12)
7. Thick, low level cloud (3)

Rocks

puzzle 30

Across
2. Turned to stone (9)
3. Remains of a plant or animal preserved in rock (6)
6. Mineral called pyrite, also known as 'fool's ___' (4)
7. Rock that has morphed, or changed (11)
8. Volcanic rock is this (7)

Down
1. Rock made of layers (11)
4. Caused when water or wind wears rocky material away (7)
5. Someone who studies rocks (11)

Super Scientists

puzzle 31

Across
2. She wrote the first computer programme (3,8)
5. Stephen ___, *A Brief History of Time* author (7)
7. This Albert said that E=MC² (8)
8. Jane ___, known for her work with chimpanzees (7)

Down
1. Michael ___, known for his work with electricity (7)
3. This Mary was a famous fossil collector (6)
4. Alexander Fleming discovered this antibiotic (10)
6. Discovered DNA with Franklin and Watson (5)

Famous Folk From History

puzzle 32

Across
1. Abraham ___, US president who abolished slavery (7)
5. Eygptian pharaoh, also known as the 'boy king' (11)
7. The only 'great' English king (6)
8. Julius ___, first dictator of the Roman Empire (7)

Down
2. Florence ___, the 'Lady with Lamp' (11)
3. Washington, Hamilton, Franklin, etc. – The ___ Fathers of the US (8)
4. Viking king who couldn't stop the tide (4)
6. Famous schoolgirl diarist from WWII (4,5)

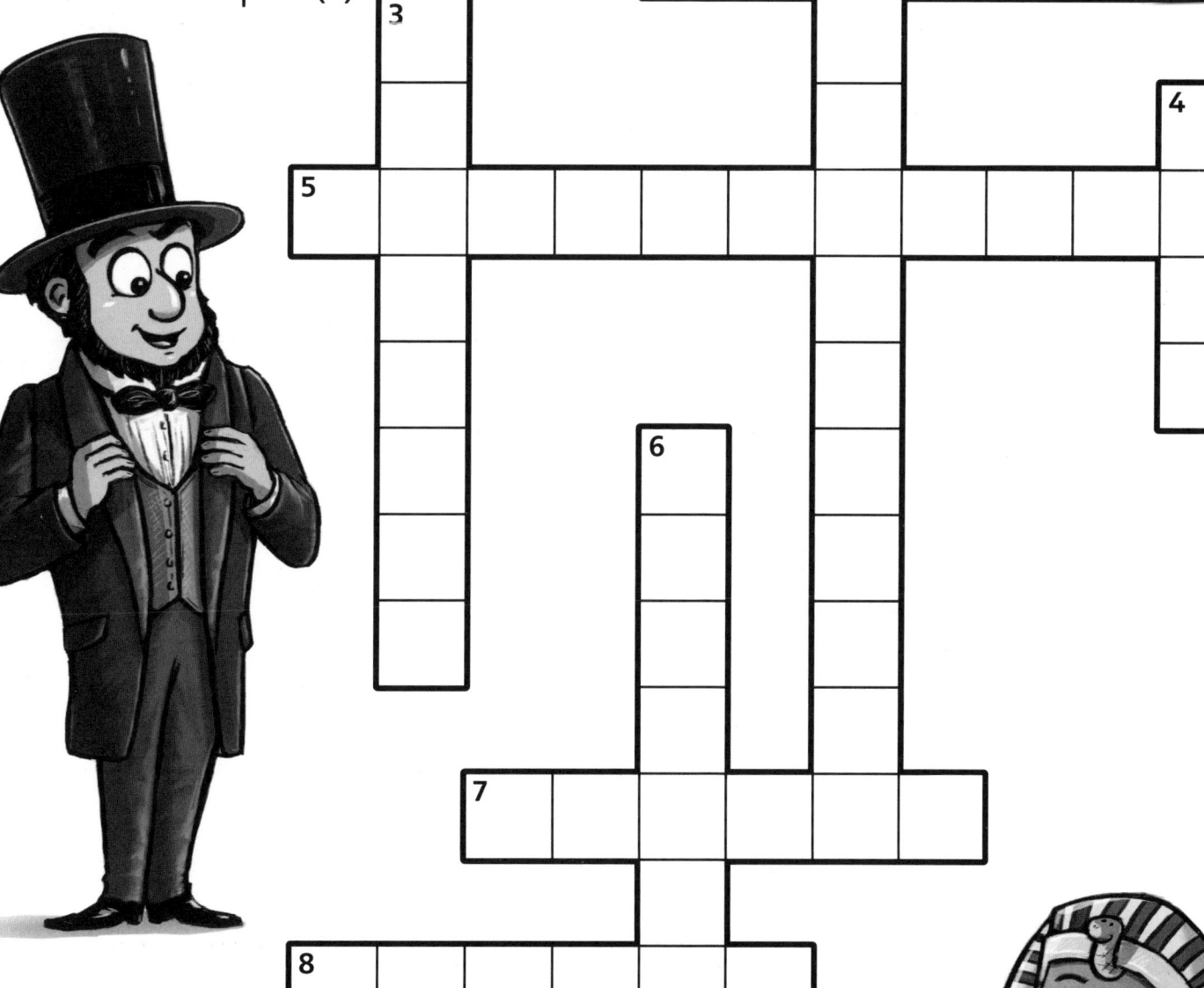

Geography

puzzle 33

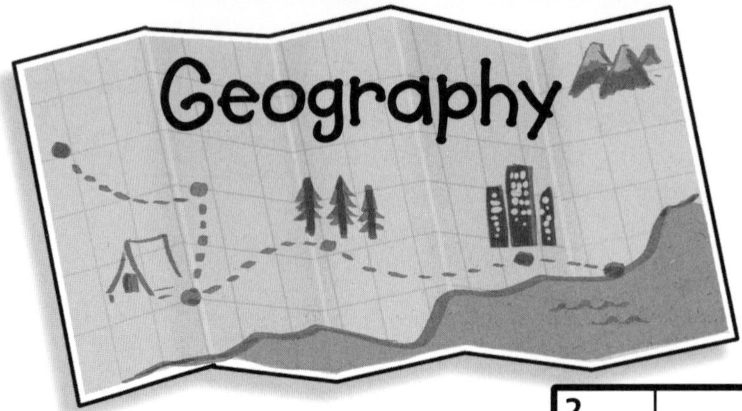

Across
2. A large area of similar ecosystems (5)
5. Map-maker (12)
7. A village, town or city, for example (10)
8. An imaginary line around the centre of the Earth (7)

Down
1. The globe can be split into two of these (11)
3. What does the G in GPS stand for? (6)
4. The region either side of the Equator (7)
6. The weather (7)

Music

puzzle 34

Across
1. Music written for a film (5)
3. The rhythm of music (4)
5. The dynamics of music refers to this (6)
6. A person who writes music (8)
7. Instruments you hit to make a sound (10)

Down
1. The lines on which musical notes sit (6)
2. The speed of a piece of music (5)
4. Composer, best known for his fifth and ninth symphonies (9)

Movers and Shakers

puzzle 35

Across
2. ___ Parks refused to give up her seat on the bus (4)
5. Martin Luther King Jr had a ___ (5)
6. Celtic Briton queen who fought the Romans (8)
8. Emmeline and Christabel ___, suffragette mother and daughter (9)

Down
1. ___ of Arc, French military leader and saint (4)
3. David ___'s *Blue Planet II* changed global thinking on plastic pollution (12)
4. Naturalist, known for his theory of evolution (6)
7. Nelson ___ fought against apartheid (7)

Back to the Future

puzzle 36

Across
1. Who was ET's human friend? (7)
3. British WWII poster – 'Keep ___ and Carry On' (4)
5. Which Kid learned to 'wax on, wax off'? (6)
6. Indiana Jones was named after his father's ___ (3)

Down
2. Doc and Marty's DeLorean car could do this (10)
3. ___ Patch Kids – must-have dolls from the 1980s (7)
4. The moonwalk is a type of ___ move (5)

Languages

puzzle 38

Across
2. People in Berlin speak this (6)
6. Hindi is spoken in this country (5)
8. A language spoken across the world (7)

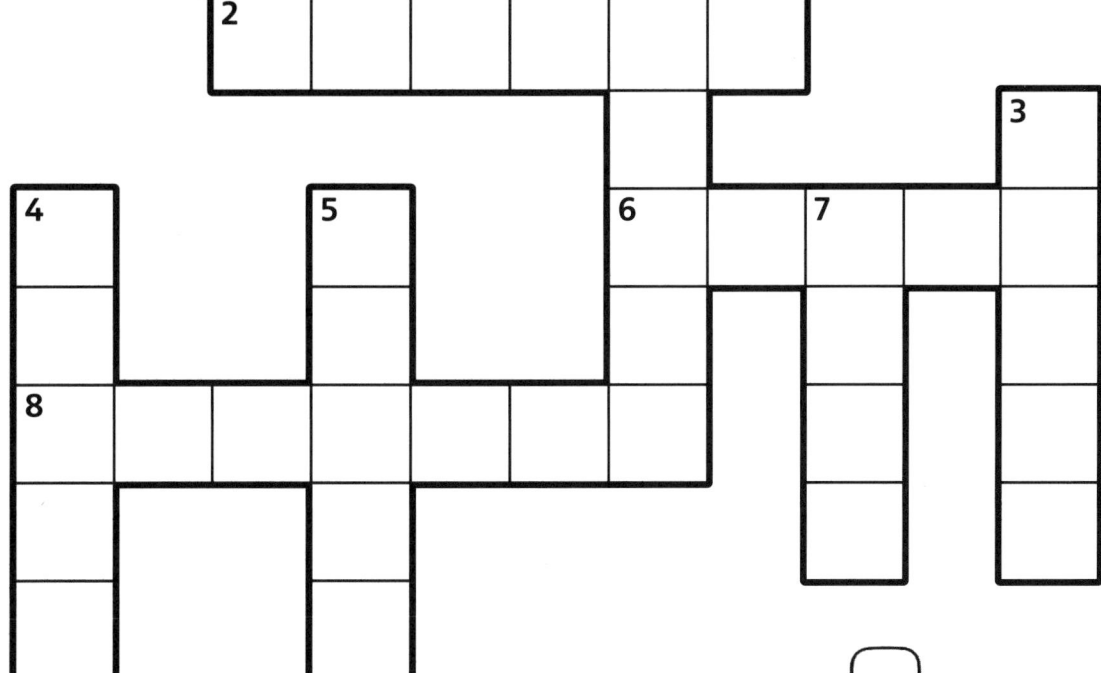

Down
1. Hola and adios mean hello and goodbye in this language (7)
3. People in Malaysia speak this language (5)
4. Spoken in Canada and France (6)
5. Someone who speaks many languages is called a what? (7)
7. Sign language helps ___ people communicate (4)

Animal Families

puzzle 39

Across
1. A group of lions (5)
3. A group of cows (4)
4. A group of sheep (5)
7. A group of bees (5)

Down
1. A group of whales (3)
2. A group of fish (5)
5. A group of rhinos (5)
6. A group of wolves (4)

Orchestra

puzzle 40

Across
2. Crash these together for effect (7)
4. Timpani, snare, kick and bass are all types of this instrument (4)
6. Play this brass instrument by moving its slide and blowing (8)
7. Blow across the mouthpiece to play this (5)

Down
1. This J-shaped woodwind instrument is made of brass (9)
2. A straight, black woodwind instrument that uses a reed (8)
3. Press the valves and blow to play this brass instrument (7)
5. A small, wooden string instrument (6)

Cities of the World

puzzle 41

Across
1. This African city could be a superhero (4,4)
5. Gladiators fought in the Colosseum here (4)
7. Home of an opera house shaped like sails (6)
8. The River Liffey is dyed green here each year on March 17th (6)
9. The 'Big Apple' (3,4)
10. Capital of the world's largest country (6)

Down
2. You'll find the Acropolis and the Parthenon here (6)
3. The 'City of Light', France (5)
4. Buckingham Palace and Trafalgar Square are here (6)
6. You might think of this New Zealand city when it rains (10)

Healthy Living

puzzle 42

Across
1. Helps keep your bones strong (7)
6. Important organ that filters your blood (5)
7. Pumps blood around your body (5)
8. ___light is a natural source of vitamin D (3)

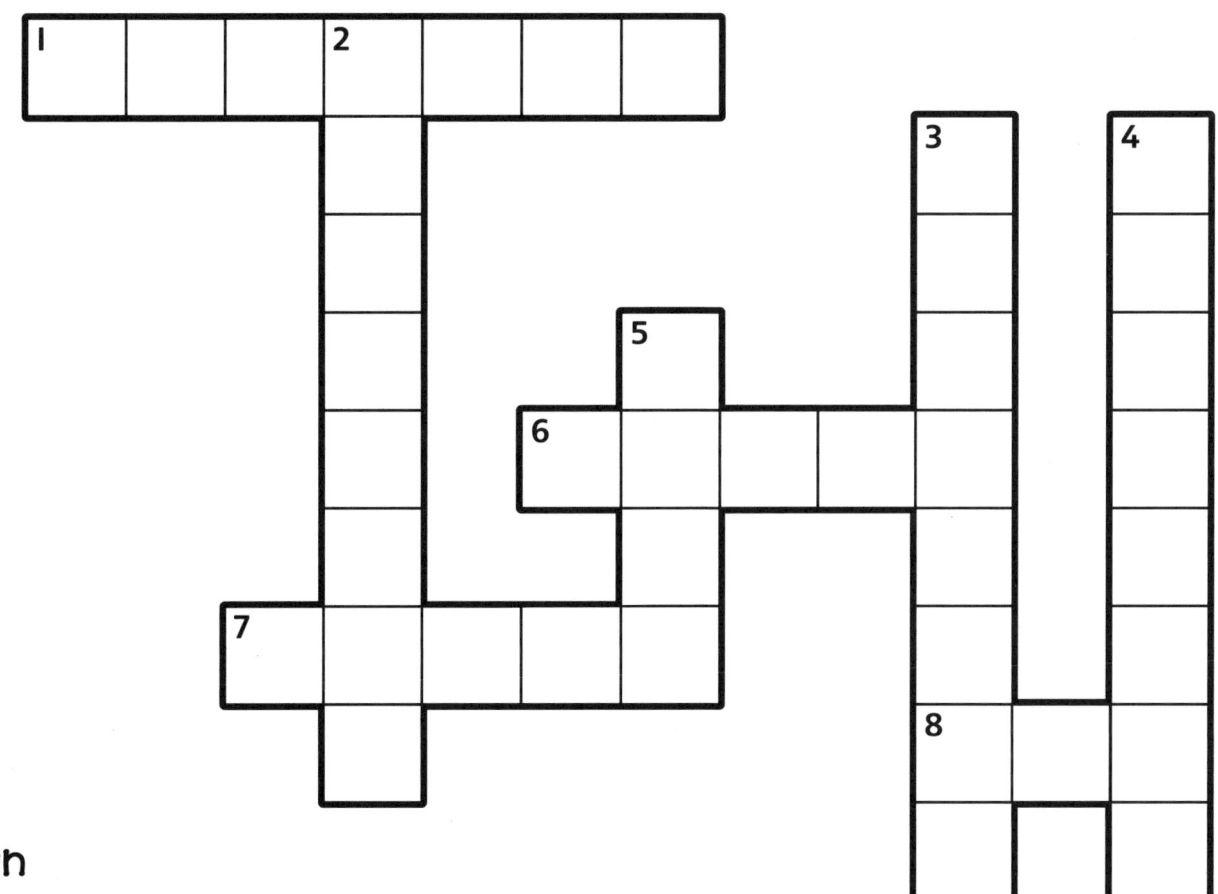

Down
2. People might count these if they are trying to lose weight (8)
3. Do this regularly to keep fit (8)
4. These come in different types – A, B, C, D, E and K (8)
5. To be healthy, you need to eat a balanced ___ (4)

Computing Conundrum

puzzle 43

Across
2. A set of rules for a computer to follow (9)
3. Data storage device (4,5)
6. Apps on a computer or tablet, for example (8)
7. To get rid of problems in a computer program (5)
8. Eight bits make up one ___ (4)

Down
1. Images are made up of these (6)
4. A giant global network of computers (8)
5. Someone who writes computer programs (5)

Myths and Legends

puzzle 44

Across
3. Boy who flew too close to the sun (6)
4. This girl opened a box and let sickness into the world (7)
5. Gorgon with snakes for hair (6)
8. Romulus and Remus were said to have been raised by these (6)

Down
1. Where Vikings go when they die (8)
2. A greedy king with a golden touch (5)
6. Odin gave one in return for wisdom (3)
7. Mischievous Norse god (4)

Awesome Authors

puzzle 45

Across
3. What is J.K. Rowling's first name? (6)
4. This Philip wrote about the *Northern Lights* (5)
6. David who knows the *World's Worst Children* (8)
8. Julia Donaldson wrote about this creature (8)

Down
1. Wrote about a chocolate factory and a fantastic fox (5,4)
2. Small creatures from J.R.R. Tolkien's books (7)
5. C.S. Lewis is associated with this piece of furniture (8)
7. Jacqueline Wilson wrote about this Tracy (6)

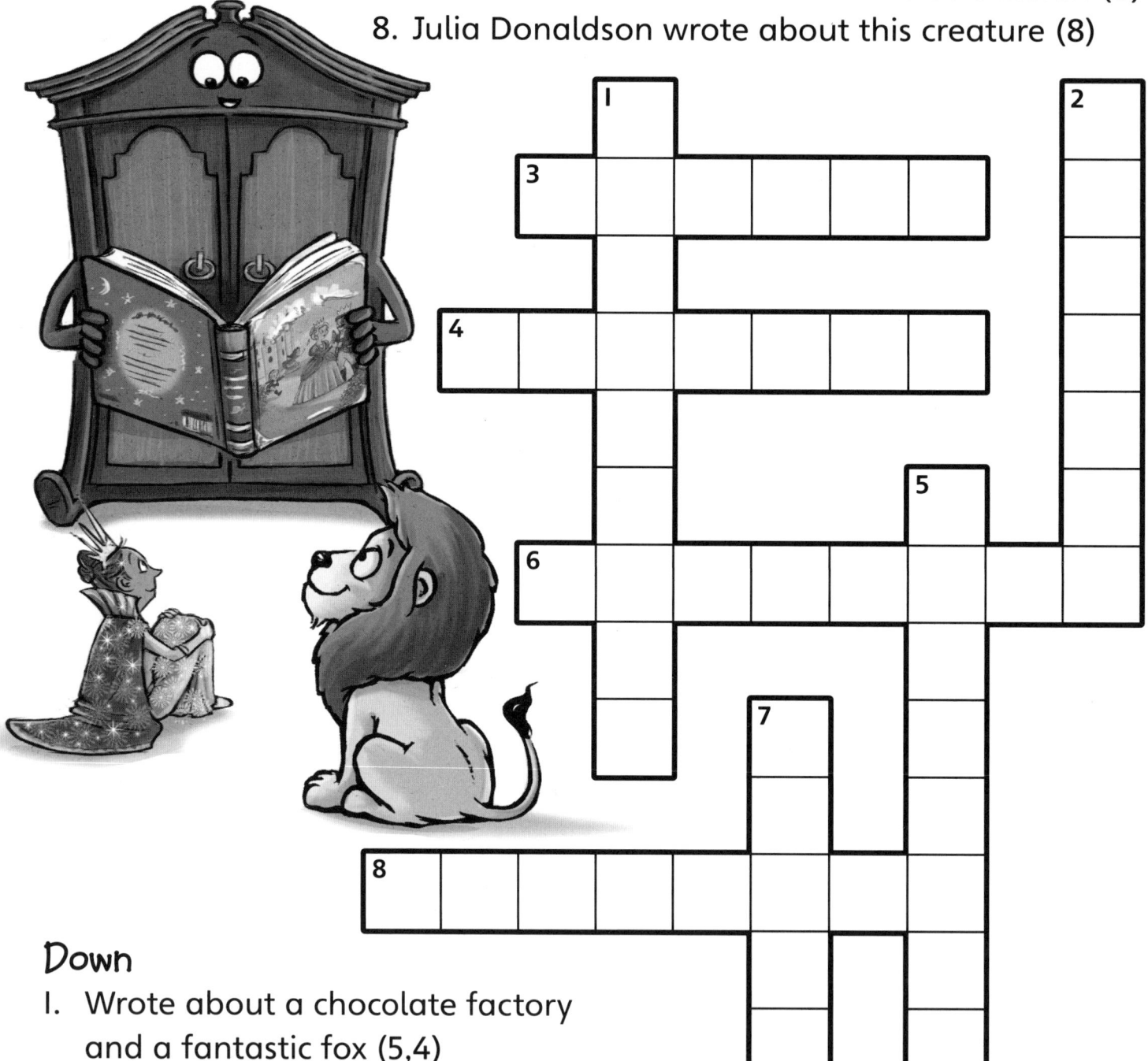

Riddle Me This

puzzle 46

Across
2. A five-letter word that becomes shorter when you add two letters to it (7)
6. What key can't open a door? (6)
7. The more you take away, the bigger it gets (4)

Down
1. What has teeth but doesn't bite? (4)
2. What is full of holes but still holds water (6)
3. This has legs but can't walk (5)
4. What goes up and down a hill but doesn't move? (4)
5. Tall when it's young, short when it's old (6)

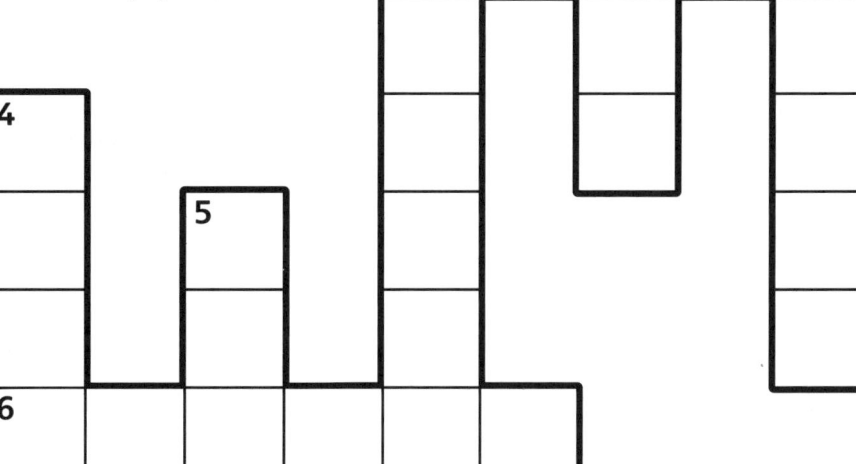

Grammar Genius

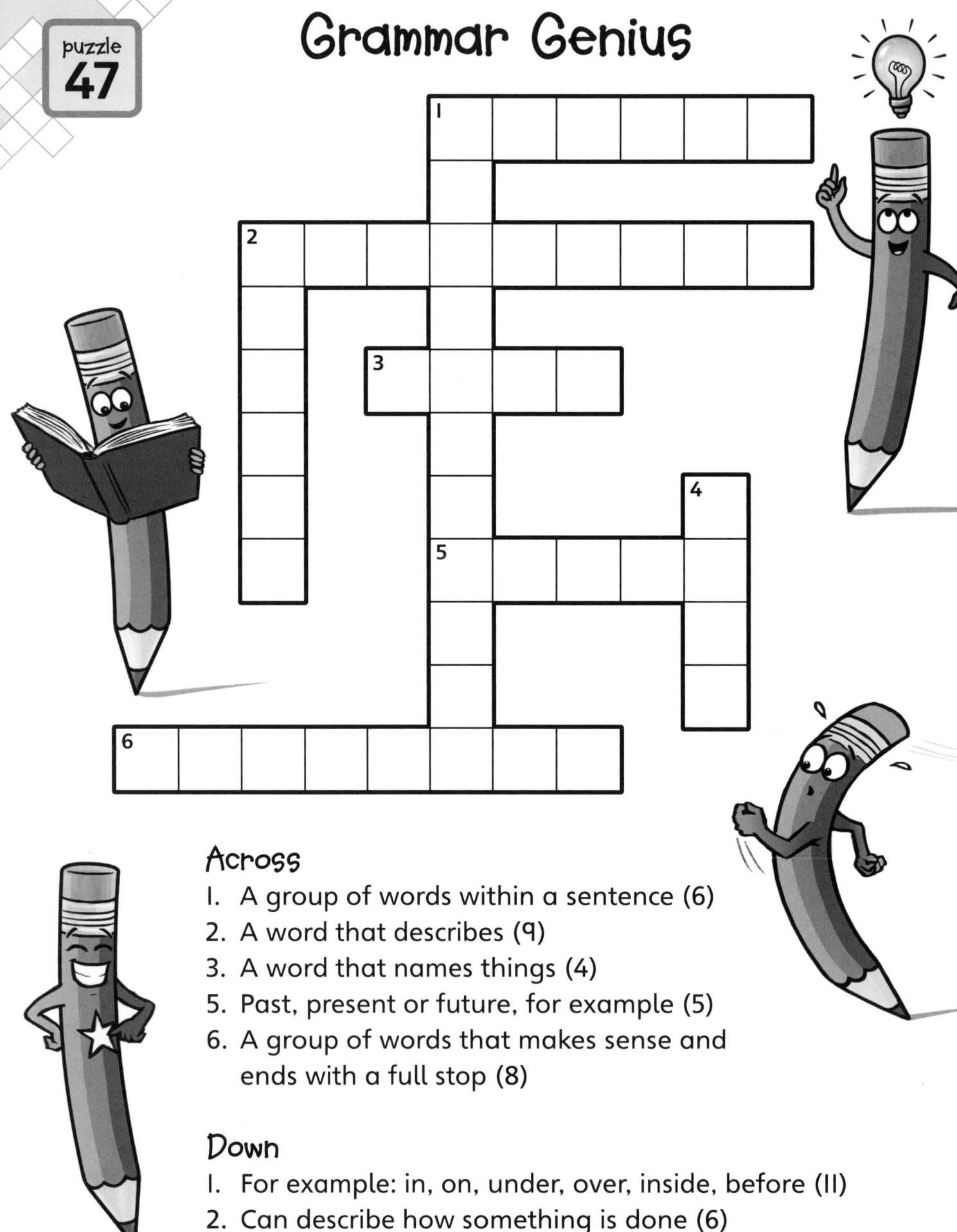

Across
1. A group of words within a sentence (6)
2. A word that describes (9)
3. A word that names things (4)
5. Past, present or future, for example (5)
6. A group of words that makes sense and ends with a full stop (8)

Down
1. For example: in, on, under, over, inside, before (11)
2. Can describe how something is done (6)
4. A 'doing' word (4)

Memorable Months

puzzle **48**

Across
2. In which month is New Year's Eve? (8)
3. The eleventh month of the year (8)
6. In which month in 1969 was the first Moon landing? (4)
8. You might fool someone at the start of this month (5)

Down
1. What month might you send a card to your love? (8)
4. In which month is Halloween celebrated? (7)
5. In the nothern hemisphere, which month has the longest day? (4)
7. In which month is World Book Day celebrated? (5)

puzzle 49

Word Links

Across
3. What links Queen Mab, Puck and Tinker Bell? (7)
5. What links toothpaste, inner and You? (4)
6. What links Dumbo, Elsa and Mickey Mouse? (6)
8. What links Raymond Briggs, Olaf and Frosty? (7)

Down
1. What links clay, Beatrix and Harry? (6)
2. What links base, foot and volley? (4)
4. What links chop, drum and hockey? (6)
7. What links Ford, Volvo and Toyota? (4)

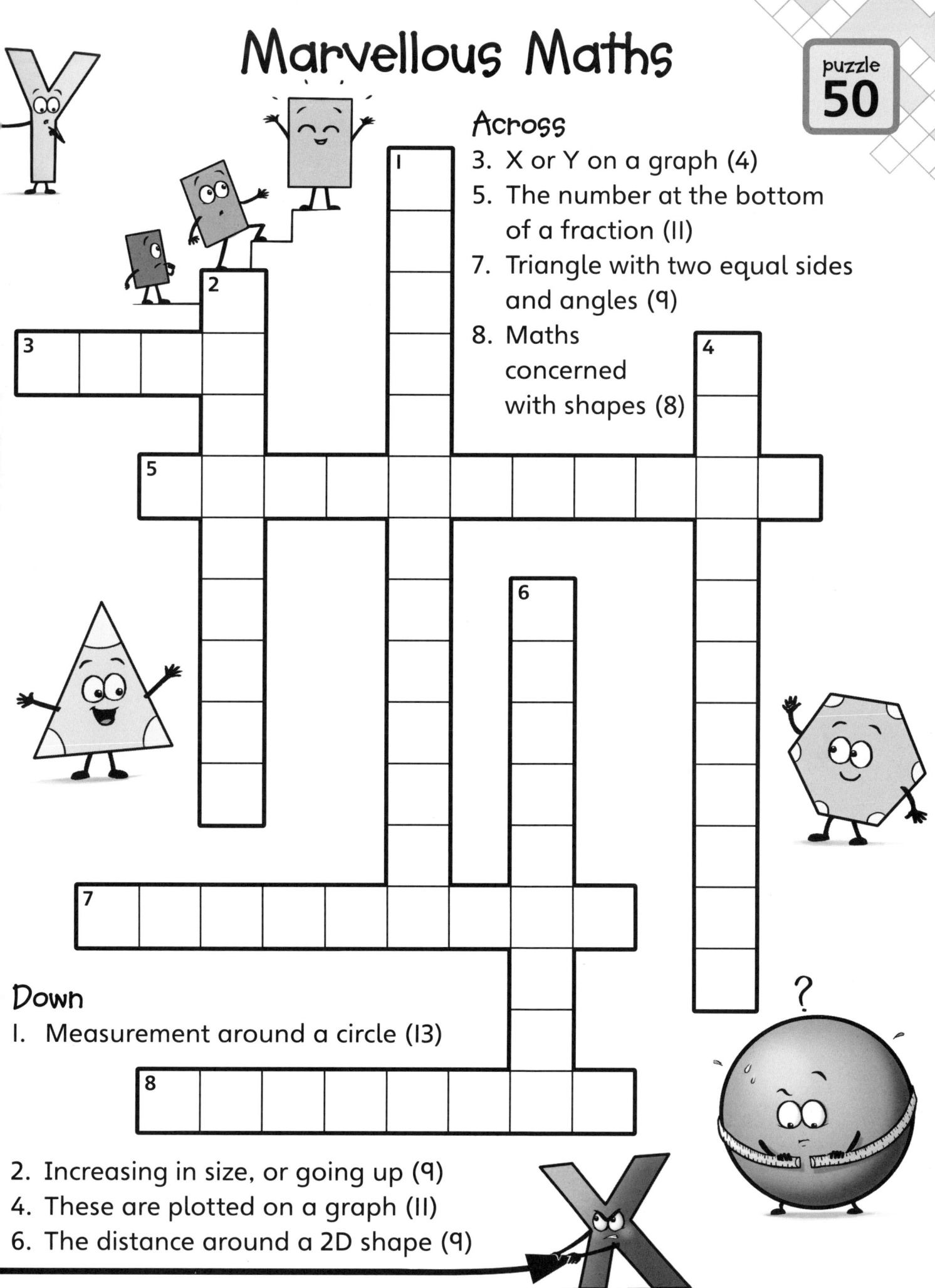

Ridiculous Riddles

puzzle 51

Across
3. What word is spelled wrong in every dictionary? (5)
4. A word that begins and ends with 'e' but only has one letter in it (8)
7. What type of cheese is made backwards? (4)
8. Has one face, two hands but no arms or legs (5)

Down
1. Break this before you can use it (3)
2. This gets wetter the more it dries (5)
5. A tree you can carry in your hand (4)
6. What has an eye but cannot see? (6)

Super Shakespeare

puzzle 52

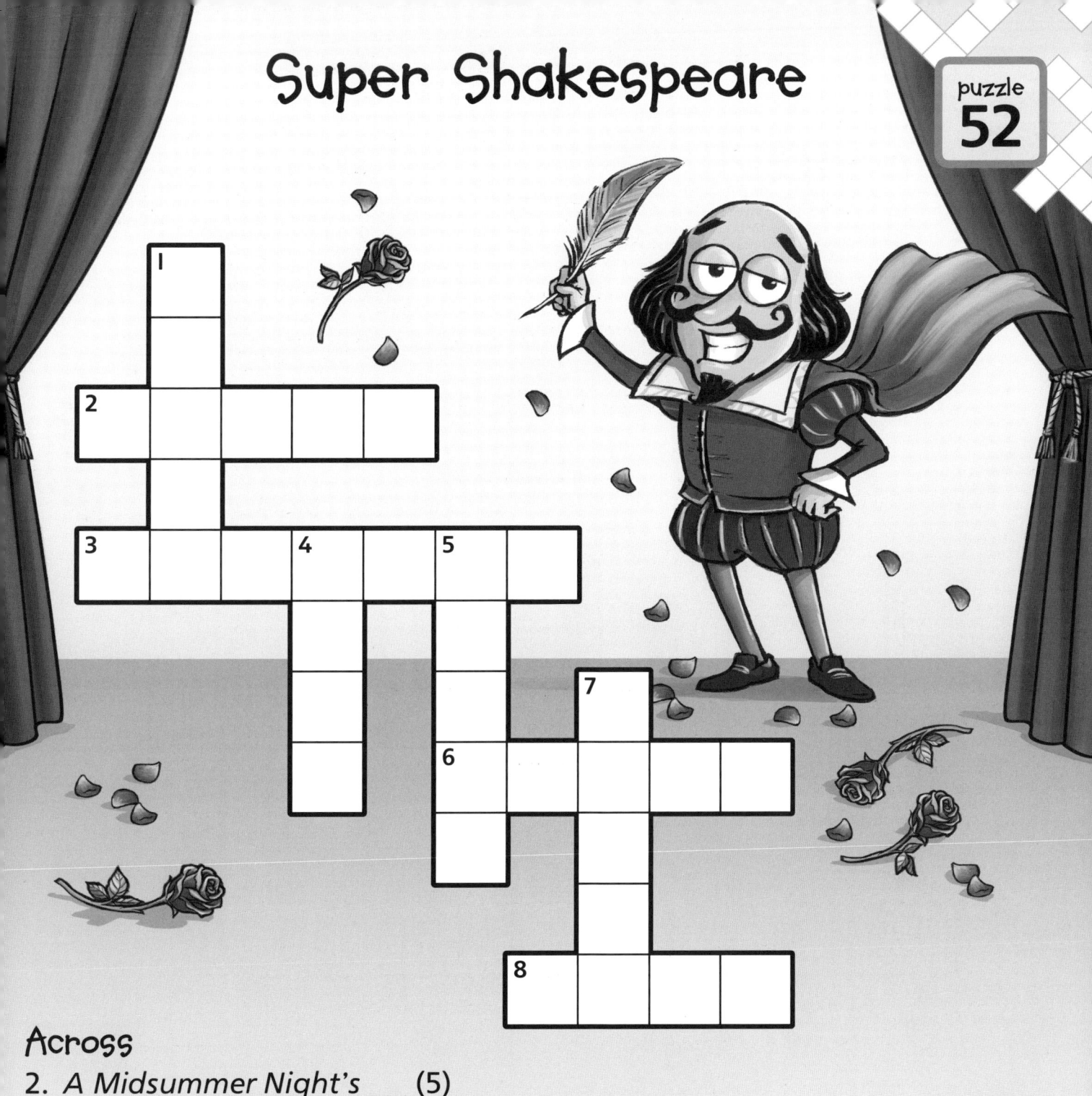

Across
2. *A Midsummer Night's ___* (5)
3. Shakespeare's last play went down a storm (7)
6. The name of Shakespeare's theatre (5)
8. "The course of true ___ never did run smooth" (4)

Down
1. How many witches were in Macbeth? (5)
4. Mischievious fairy, also known as Robin Goodfellow (4)
5. "All the world's a ___" (5)
7. Juliet fell in love with him (5)

Peculiar Plurals

puzzle 53

Across
1. More than one woman (5)
5. More than one thief (7)
7. More than one louse (4)
8. More than one person (6)

Down
2. More than one moose (3)
3. More than one octopus (6)
4. More than one goose (5)
6. More than one sheep (6)

Who Said that?

puzzle 54

Across
3. "You're a wizard, Harry!" (6)
7. "To die would be an awfully big adventure!" (5,3)
8. "Curiouser and curiouser." (5)

Down
1. "Don't gobblefunk around with words." (3)
2. "Please, sir, I want some more." (6,5)
4. "Do you want to build a snowman?" (4)
5. "There's no place like home." (7)
6. "A spoonful of sugar helps the medicine go down." (4,7)

Terrific Technology

puzzle 55

Across
2. With this you can make calls anywhere (6,5)
5. A ___ oven heats your food with tiny waves (9)
6. The kind of press invented by Gutenberg in the 15th century (8)
8. Dr Who has a sonic one (11)

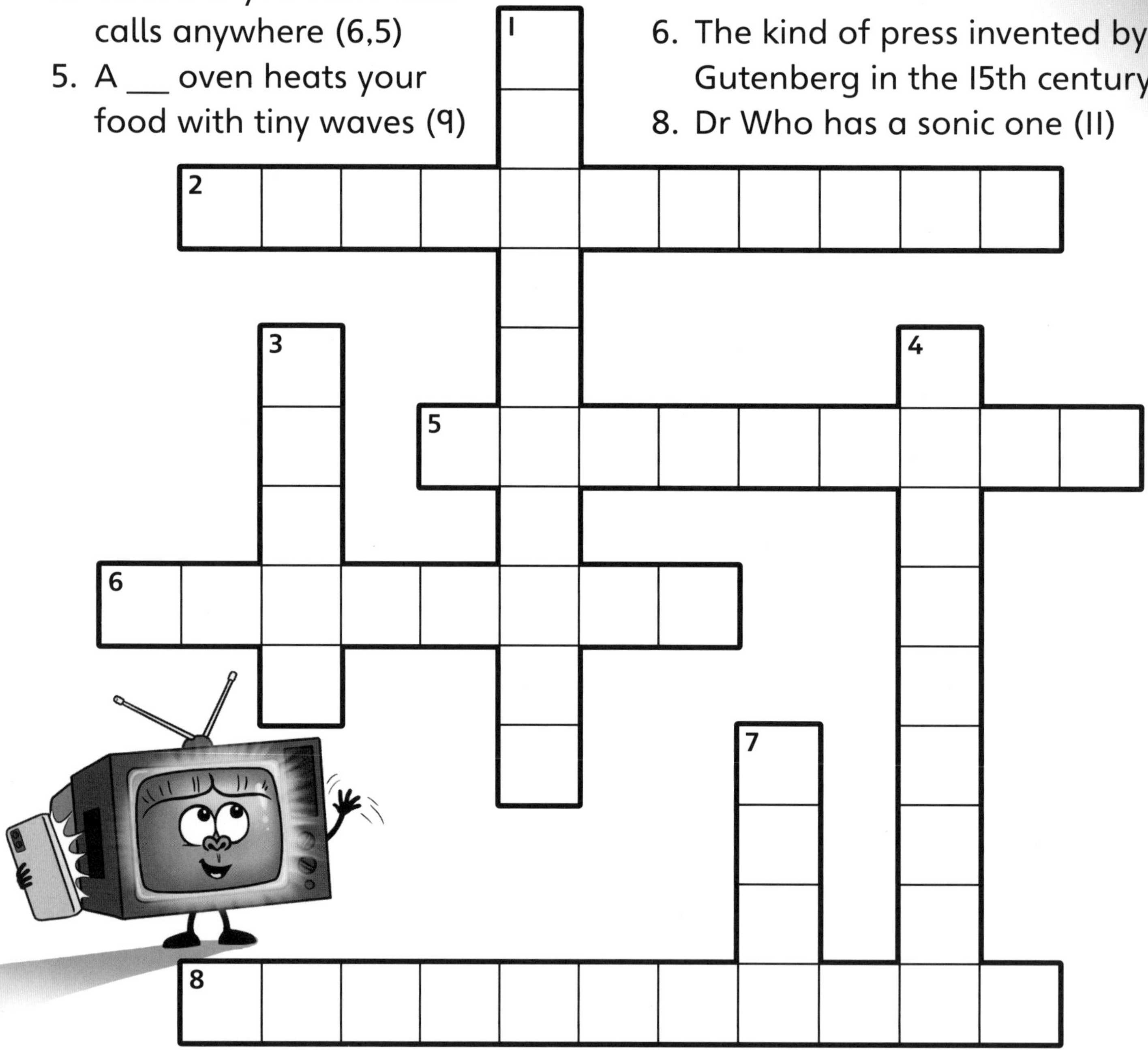

Down
1. Originally only black-and-white, now in HD and 8K (10)
3. Tune in to listen and go Ga Ga for this (5)
4. Needed for GPS and mobile phones to work (9)
7. Use this to get online without wires (4)

Kings and Queens

puzzle 56

Across
4. He was all shook up in Graceland (5)
5. This hairy King climbed the Empire State Building (4)
7. This stellar queen had children called Luke and Leia (5)
8. Hans Christian Andersen's wintery queen (4)

Down
1. This queen often said, "Off with their heads!" (5,2,6)
2. ___ the Conqueror, the first Norman king of England (5)
3. The Lion King (5)
6. Fairy queen in *A Midsummer Night's Dream* (7)

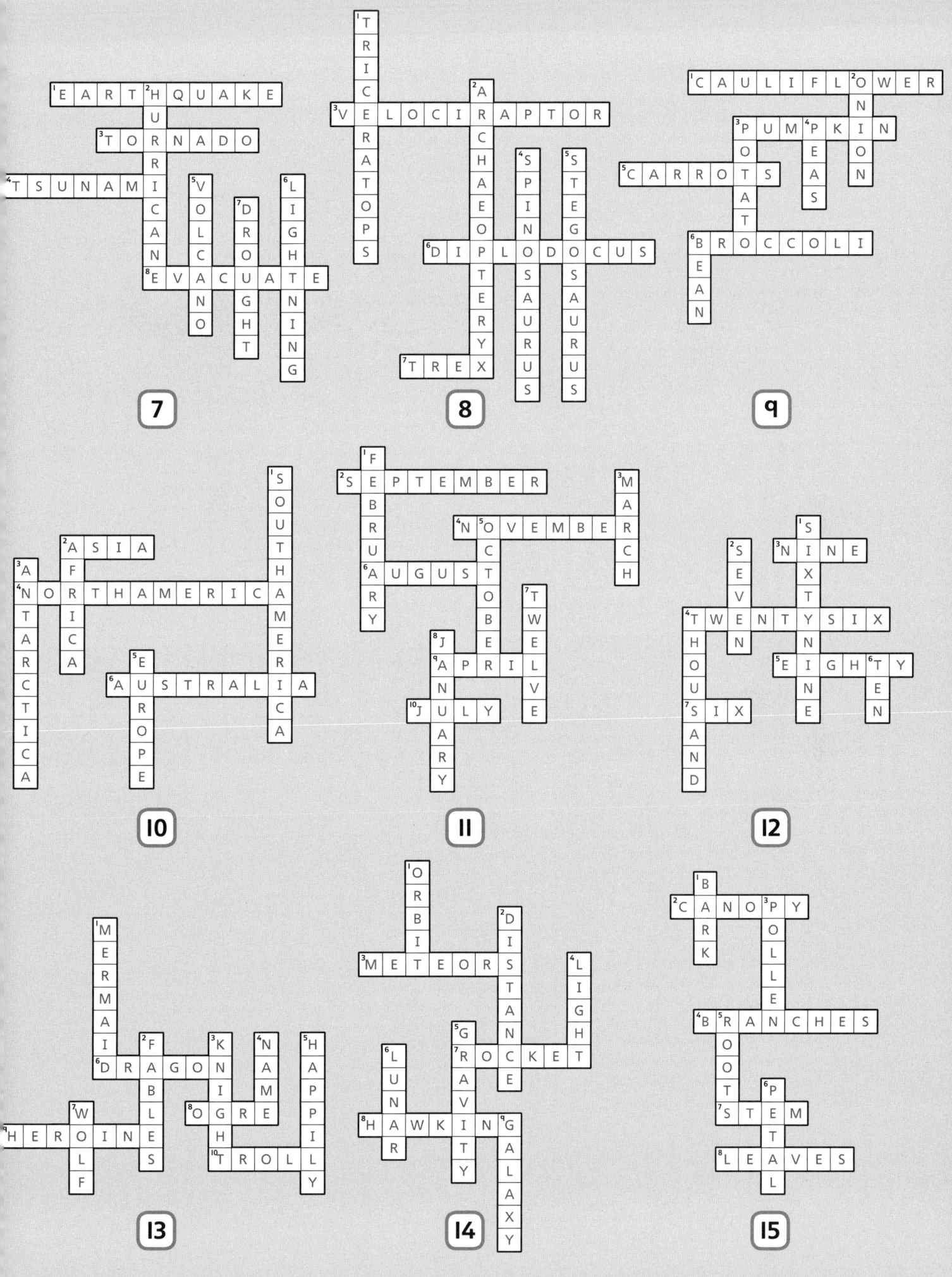

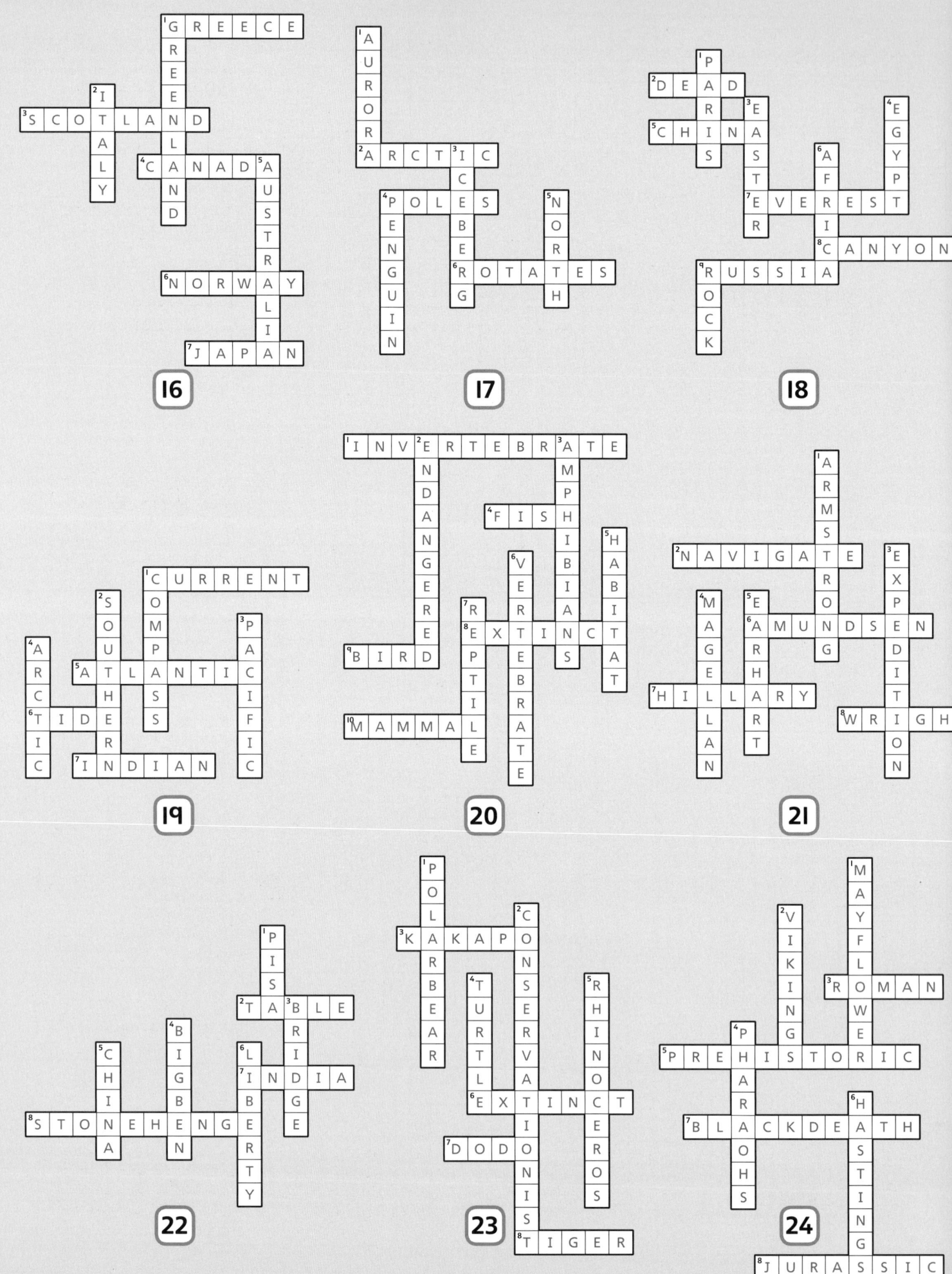

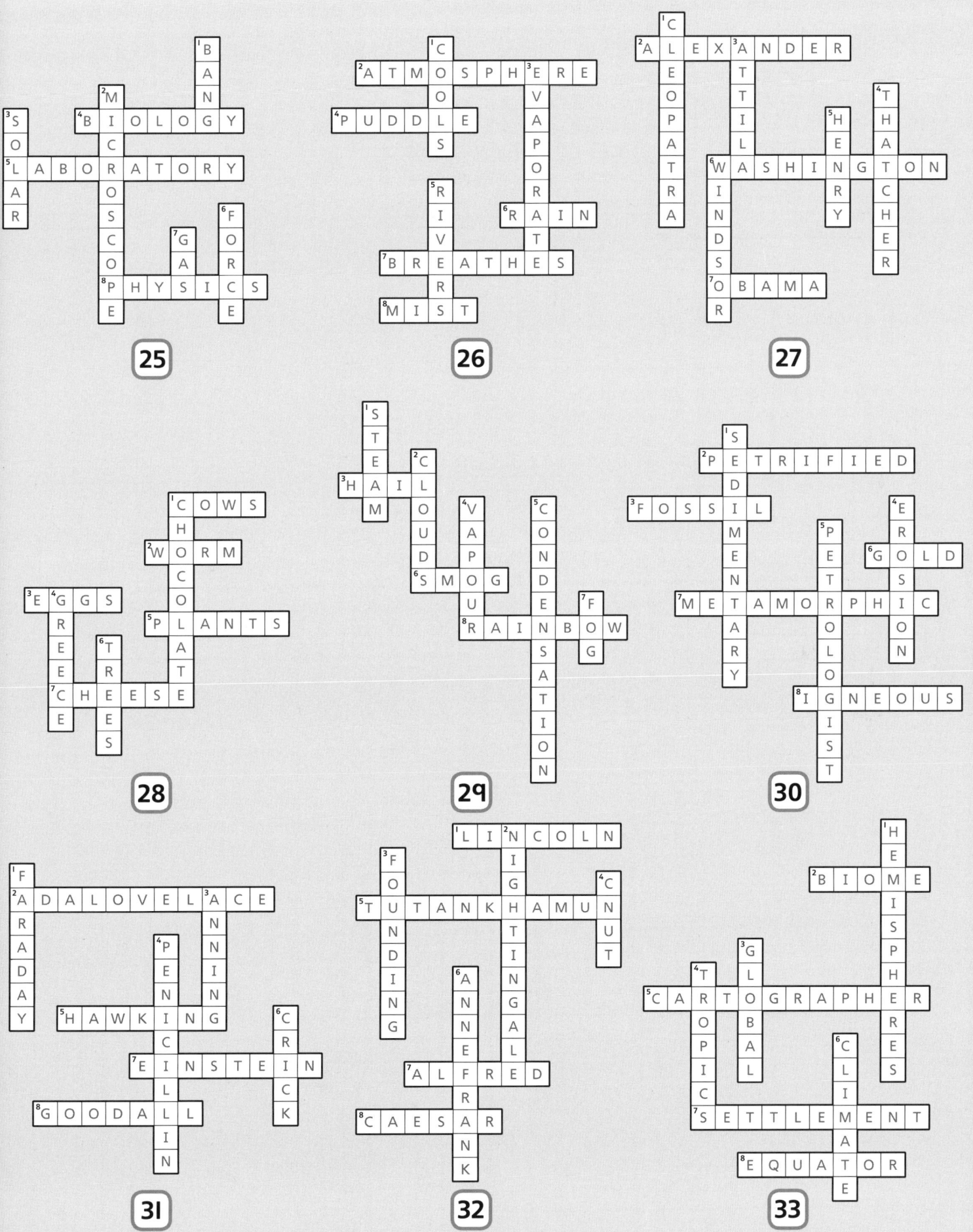

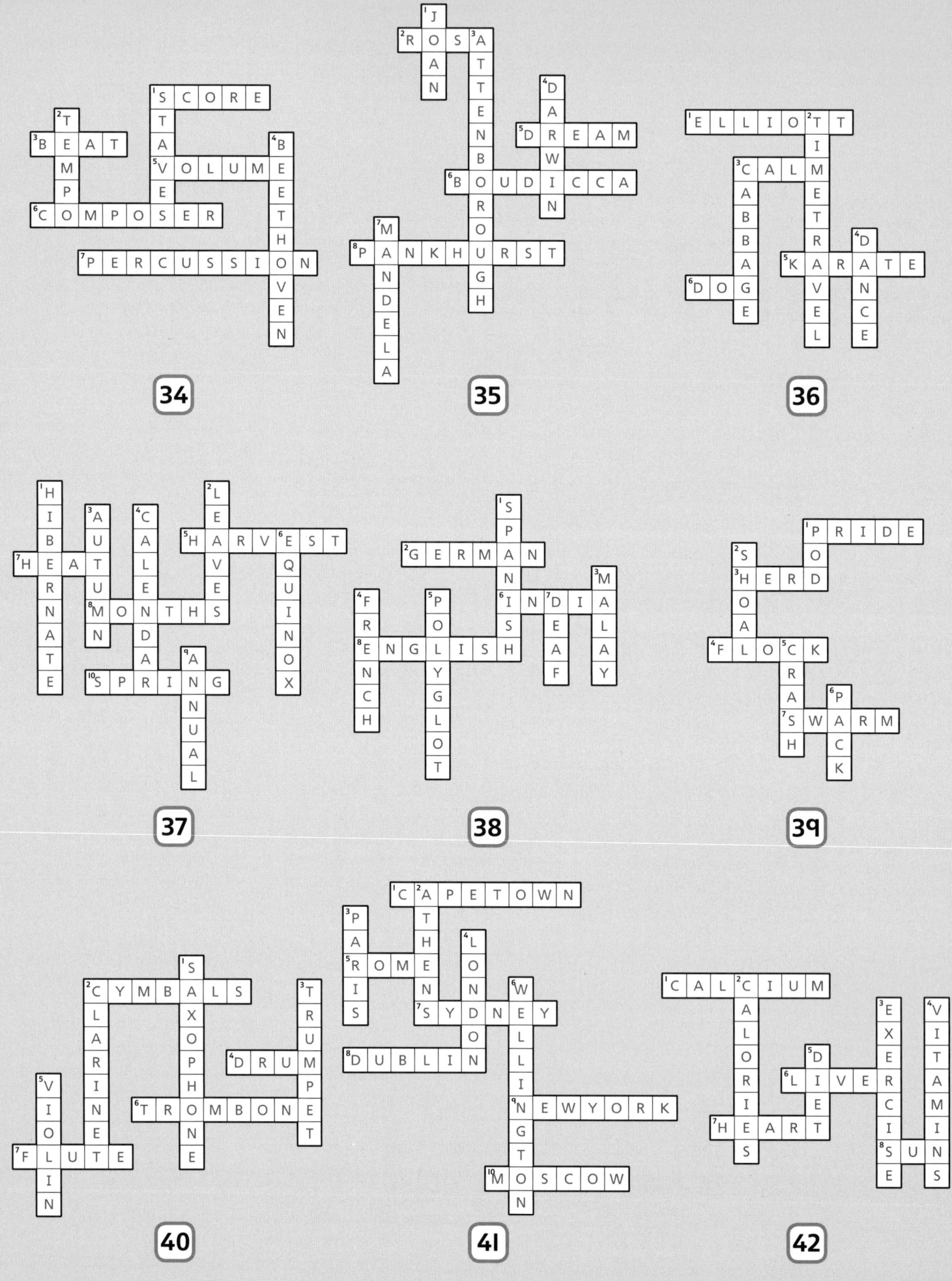

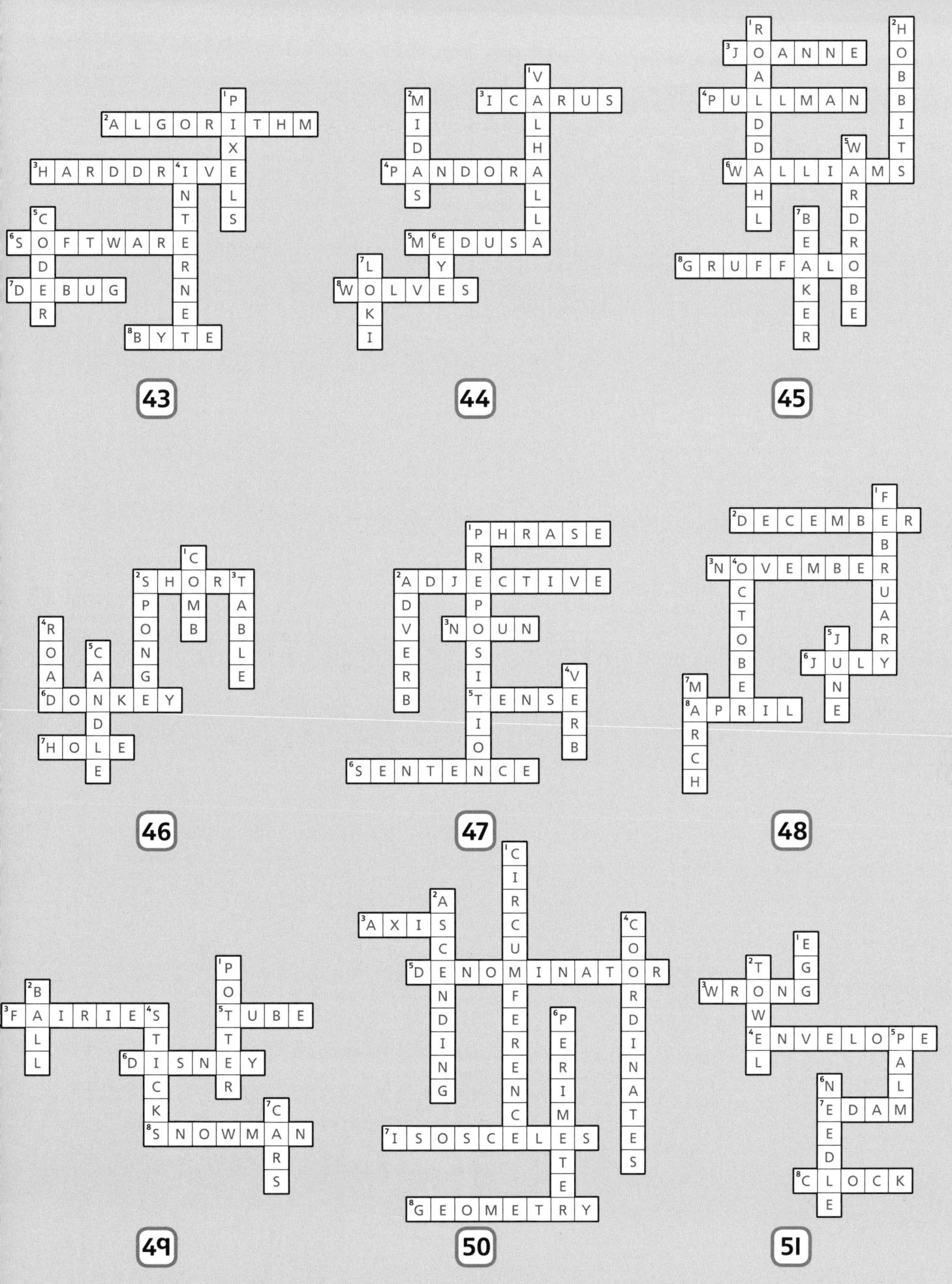